When Paul Met Artie

When Paul Met Artie

The Story of Simon & Garfunkel

G. NERI illustrated by DAVID Litchfield

CANDLEWICK PRESS

Old Friends *SEPTEMBER 19, 1981*

At dawn,
people hit the streets
all over New York City,
making their way
into the heart
of the weary metropolis —
Central Park.
Despite the gray skies
and morning drizzle,
the city comes to life —
horns blaring,
drivers shouting,
subway trains rumbling
underfoot —
a symphony
of noise.

Deep in the quiet
of the once great park,
away from all the hustle
and bustle of the city,
people of all kinds
are gathering —
singles, couples, families,
young and old,
rich and poor —
they're all here
in anticipation of
the Big Event.

They bring blankets and food,
Frisbees and guitars,
and, most important,
boom boxes and radios
to listen to the delicate and
haunting sounds
of two voices singing
in perfect harmony.

All week long,
those two voices
have filled the airwaves
from Forest Hills
to Greenwich Village,
cascading out of cars and cafés,
apartments and stores alike.
Two voices
sounding like
autumn and spring
rolled into one,
like snowflakes
falling on barren trees,
or the joyous dance
of summer in the park.
Two voices intertwining,
birds soaring in flight,
pure harmony,
pure delight.
Two voices for the city
of New York.

At dusk, the clouds
magically part, shining sunlight
on half a million people —
more than this great town
has *ever* seen in one place —
as they wait
for a homecoming
like no other.

When two lone figures,
one tall and lanky
with light curly locks,
the other short and trim
with dark straight hair,
finally take the stage,
an endless sea of faces
greets them with a
rapturous roar.
It has been more than ten years
since these hometown heroes
went their separate ways.
"It's great to do
a neighborhood concert,"
says the one with the guitar,
beaming.
"I'm soo in the mood," says
the curly-haired fellow
with a laugh.

Just like old times.

My Little Town *THIRTY YEARS EARLIER...*

At the end of the subway line,
deep in the Jewish suburbs
of Queens,
everything looks the same.
Cookie-cutter row houses
with orange rooftops, brick veneer,
and hedges perfectly trimmed.
The only way to tell them apart
is by the family car
in every driveway.
Every deli brims with Yiddish
and knishes;
every Shabbat dinner, gefilte fish
and challah bread.
The women wear scarves or hats
with their dresses;

the men, vested suits and fedoras.
And on Sunday drives,
everyone listens
to the same bland music:
happy-go-lucky pop tunes,
loopy polkas, and sappy
love songs.

In this world of sameness,
two boys, born
three weeks apart,
grow up a few blocks
from each other
in a neighborhood
called Kew Gardens Hills.
The two boys are

opposites
in every way.
One tall, one short.
One lefty, one righty.
One with light curly hair,
one a black straight mop.
One with a head for math,
one for jokes.
One a Philadelphia Phillies fan,
one a die-hard Yankee.

The tall boy
grooves to his own tune—
a pitch-perfect singer
at nine years old.
Crooning alone

in the school stairwell,
he listens to his voice
echo and bounce off the walls.
The sound gives him
goose bumps.
His voice is his only friend.
It keeps him company,
makes him feel lucky
to have such a gift.
On his way home,
marching along
to the tempo of a song
and singing out loud
in higher and higher keys,
he gets odd looks
from the other boys.

But the neighborhood mothers
pause to listen—
it's the highlight of their day.
To them, he is The Voice.
His real name is
Artie Garfunkel.

For the smaller boy,
the sound of baseball
is music to his ears.
The crack of the bat and
the roar of the crowd
are better than any music
on the radio.
On his bike,
he cruises the neighborhoods,

a chip on his shoulder
from being called "shorty,"
chasing down games of stickball
to prove he's as big
as his heroes,
the New York Yankees.
"Hey, Slugger!"
his brother calls him,
because he bats
just like the great
Mickey Mantle.
Whack! He can hit too.
His real name is Paul Simon.

Paul and Artie
have never met.

The Only Living Boy in New York

Paul has seen Artie
around the neighborhood,
wearing a red Phillies cap
or shaking boxes of Good & Plenty
in the candy store.
But until he sees Artie
standing nervously onstage
at the fourth-grade talent show,
Paul hasn't given him
a second thought.
But then again,
neither has anyone else
at school.

That is, until
Artie opens his mouth
and out pours
The Voice:
smooth,
hypnotic,
and sounding

just like the unforgettable
Nat King Cole himself.
Paul can't believe
what he's hearing.
He's spent plenty of time
down at the Roseland Ballroom,
listening to his dad,
a bass player and leader
of a big-time swing band,
so he knows talent
when he sees it.
This kid Artie is like
a human jukebox,
his voice casting a spell
over the entire school auditorium.
When he hits the final note,
it hangs in the air,
sucking the breath
out of everyone in attendance.
There is a moment of silence —
then the crowd of grade-schoolers
erupts with cheers.

Stunned, Paul looks
all around him.
This morning nobody knew
who this kid was.
Now everyone is talking
about Artie.
Paul longs to hold
an audience spellbound too,
to have his moment
in the spotlight
when everyone
is talking about him
for once.

*Singing. That's
where it's at,* he thinks.
*If that kid can do it,
maybe I can too.*

Someday.

Two Teen-Agers

"How would you like to be
a rabbit?" the teacher asks Paul,
out of desperation.
He has become a handful in school,
the class clown, seeker
of attention.
So he's drafted to play
the White Rabbit
in the sixth-grade production
of *Alice in Wonderland.*
The role is a perfect fit —
rambunctious
and full of nervous energy.
What makes him say yes
is the guy who's playing
the Cheshire Cat:
that kid from the talent show,
Artie.
To perform on the same stage
as The Voice?
If I can impress him and
become his friend,
maybe some of that magic
will rub off on me,
Paul thinks.
Determined, he goes home
and starts singing along
to his record of
Alice in Wonderland songs.
Over and over he croons.

It's like swinging a bat —
he misses, flubs it, tries again.
Determined, he slowly gets
better and better,
trying out different songs,
singing in the bathroom,
listening to the echo of his voice
bouncing off the tiles
until he connects.
There's a knock on the door.
"You have a real nice voice, Paul,"
says his musical dad.
Base hit.

Artie sits offstage,
watching Paul get ready
to rehearse his scene.
He's noticed Paul before,
taking command of the
schoolyard ball games.
But today, Paul seems
out of his element.
He's so nervous, he starts
cracking jokes left and right,
making faces and pulling pranks.
He scrambles through his scene,
milking every last laugh
and looking Artie's way
for a reaction.
Artie is practically crying

from laughing so hard.
Home run.

Artie gives him the nod of approval
and they spend the coming days
goofing around, flipping cards, and
imitating the teacher behind her back.
Since they live in the same neighborhood,
they soon find themselves
walking home together.
When Paul pulls out his Yankees cap,
Artie pulls out his Phillies cap.
Pretty daring to wear the hat of a rival
in this neighborhood.
Artie shrugs. "I'm a lefty and lefties
like to throw curveballs."
Paul laughs. He likes that Artie
goes his own way.

Artie invites him over
to his house,
where they goof around on
his dad's tape recorder, taking turns
imitating corny pop songs
and yukking it up
with their shtick.
For now,
Alice in Wonderland can wait.
The Paul and Artie Show
is a hit.

Dancing Wild

Banished.
That's how the boys feel
when they are both sent
to a gifted junior high school
in the rough part of Queens.
To get there, they must cross
ten blocks of enemy territory
where bullies are always itching
for a fight.
Almost every week
Paul and Artie get beat up
or have their lunch money taken.
They come home,
books muddied,
clothes ripped,
defeated.

Everything is changing.
Both boys turn thirteen—
the year of their bar mitzvahs,
the year they're declared
young men.
Paul has become moody,
tired of seeing everyone
grow taller than him.
Only Artie has his back.
They become best pals,
retreating from all the other kids.

But even this gloomy cloud
has a silver lining.

In a supermarket parking lot,
Paul sits in his parents' car,
flipping through radio stations
in search of anything worth
listening to.
He's bored with what passes for
music on the radio;
all he finds is
the squeaky-clean Doris Day
or the cute Patti Page
or the easy-on-the-ears Perry Como.
Then suddenly,
through the static,
his ears are assaulted
by a wail unlike anything
he's ever heard before.

The howl makes his legs
twitch.
The yowl makes him want
to scream and shout.
The piercing sound feels like a blast
from the future and even has
an alien name: Elvis.
For one minute and fifty-eight seconds,
Paul feels like he's on
the Coney Island roller coaster,
a whirlwind of emotion whipping
his moodiness away.
When the song is over,
he has to catch his breath.

Whatever that was,
I want to take that ride again.

At school, Artie finds
a mysterious note:
Listen to Moondog's
Rock 'n' Roll Party *tonight!*
Intrigued, he tunes in to WINS,
and out of his cream-colored
plastic radio comes:
Get ready to SHAKE!
Get ready to JUMP!
Get ready to DANCE your heart away!
It's time to turn UP the volume
for Moondog's Rock 'n' Roll Party*!*
Music erupts from the speakers—
the room shakes, rattles, and rolls.
Artie's never heard anything like it.
Not at school,
not on variety shows,
and definitely not on the radio.
This is something different,
something alive,
something rebellious.

He can't stop
listening.

We've Got a Groovy Thing Goin'

Artie, who's something
of a math geek,
spends weeks charting
the rise and fall of popular songs
on *Your Hit Parade*.
To him, listening to rock 'n' roll
on the radio
is like belonging
to a secret club —
four hours of rebellion a night

against the blandness
all around them.
*How much fun would it be
if we could sing
on the radio too?*
he thinks.

The boys lock themselves
in Artie's basement,
singing their favorite songs
into the recorder.
But Paul doesn't sound like Elvis,
and Artie's voice isn't bluesy
like Johnny Ace's.
They don't have a band like
the Crew Cuts or Bill Haley
and His Comets.
They're just two voices
and a tape recorder.

Artie has an idea:
maybe he can chart the rise
and fall
of their voices
just like he charts the hits.
Dissecting the top tunes
to see what makes them tick,
Artie figures out how
their voices can work
together.
When he takes the high
tenor melody, and Paul
the low-scale harmony,
something *clicks*.
It reminds Paul of his dad
tuning his bass guitar:
when two strings come into focus,
they suddenly resonate
as one.
When the boys sing into
that harmonic sweet spot,
they're giddy
with laughter.
Two voices are better
than one.

For months,
that's all they do —
sit nose to nose
in the basement,
practicing every sound
until it's perfect.
They record themselves
to hear their flaws
until there aren't any left.
They sing along
to their good takes,
recording their live voices
against their taped voices
to create a *four*-part
harmony.
With two Pauls and
two Arties singing,
they're now *twice*
as good.

As Artie listens to their recordings
over and over, one thing is clear.
When he sang in synagogue,
his angelic voice made
grown men cry.
But singing with Paul is different.
It grooves. It swings.
When he turns up the volume,
it rattles the walls.

This is rock 'n' roll.

I Am a Rock

Paul doesn't want to be
Mickey Mantle anymore—
he wants to be
a rock 'n' roll star.
Even though his dad
hates Elvis and all the rest,
he gives Paul
a guitar for his thirteenth birthday,
thinking it might be good
for him to learn
an instrument.

Paul teaches himself how to play
"Rudolph the Red-Nosed Reindeer"—
only like Elvis would:
hair slicked back, collar up,
hips shaking.
The other thing shaking
is his dad's head when he realizes
all Paul cares about
is rock 'n' roll.
When Paul asks him
how to play a new radio hit
called "Earth Angel,"
his dad shows him
the five basic chords
in every rock 'n' roll song.
For Paul, it's like the floodgates
open.

He grabs Artie at school the next day:
"Look at this! All these songs
use the same chords!"
Set free by this magic formula,
Paul strums every day
till his fingers
are raw.
They're one step closer
to becoming a real band.

Unfortunately,
with the gift of those five chords,
his dad has created
a monster.
Paul and his guitar
become inseparable.
Even when he and Artie
get into trouble at school,
they turn the detention room
into their own private
rock 'n' roll party.
Every evening,
Paul locks himself in his room,
learning new songs by
Elvis or Chuck Berry.

"You play that thing six hours a day
instead of studying. That music's
awful!" his dad yells.
Paul can't believe he,
of all people,
doesn't understand.
Meanwhile,
Artie's mom worries that
her son wants to be a musician
instead of something
respectable
like a lawyer.
But it's too late.
Paul and Artie
are the only ones
who recognize that
everything has changed.

You Can Tell the World

Scoping out the crowd
at the last dance
of junior high school,
Artie and Paul both feel nervous.
They know what
they need to do:
create magic.
They saw it once before
when they snuck off to see a
Moondog rock 'n' roll show
in Brooklyn—
there was Little Richard,
standing on a piano in a cape,
dancing and wailing
like he owned the world.
Rock 'n' roll live was *way* better
than they'd imagined.
Now if only
they could do *that*.

It's a perfect, crisp night,
the starry skies sparkling overhead.
Students are milling about,
waiting for the music
to begin.
Gathering his courage,
Paul nods to Artie.
The time is now.
Walking together
into the middle of the crowd,
they clear a space.
They have no band,
just Paul's guitar

and their voices.
Paul counts off, and
Artie's high, sweet voice
launches into a series
of outlandish sounds—
*ding-dong*s, *allang*s,
and *ba-doodle-ay*s.
Kids are craning their necks
to see what's going on
when Paul comes in with
his warm, soft voice, crooning
to a song called "Sh-Boom."
When their harmonies kick in,
it's like a bomb
drops into the middle
of the schoolyard—
shhhh-BOOOM!
They set the song free
with their unique sound.
The crowd, growing bigger,
sways in unison,
snapping their fingers
to the catchy beat.
Before Paul and Artie even hit
their final note,
whistles, hoots, and hollers break out.
Paul and Artie
are the hit
of the evening.
Heading into high school,
the boys are finally
in the spotlight
together.

Our Song

The summer
of their fourteenth year,
the whole city comes alive
with harmony.
Paul and Artie hear it
on street corners,
in tunnels and stairwells,
parks and playgrounds.
People will soon call it *doo-wop*—
the sound of five-person vocal groups
taking over the neighborhoods
with their infectious harmonies.
Dooo-wop-wop! Dooo-wop-wop!
No stage or band needed.
Just a street corner, your friends,
and a song
to stake your claim
as the best singers
on the block.

Wanting in on the action,
the boys recruit three other friends
and form their own gang,
the Peptones.
Harmonizing under streetlights
on sultry summer nights with
a lead, bass, falsetto,
and backup vocals,
they're willing to throw down
the gauntlet
against any other crew.

The only thing missing—
their own songs.

Since doo-wop is all about
young love—
something Paul and Artie
have yet to fully experience—
they write about their dream girl,
taking turns as the words
come tumbling out—
visions of a girl
with a flower in her hair.
A girl who will always
be true and always be there.
That's the girl for them.
And with the vision of that girl
they dream up
their very first song.

Unsure if "The Girl for Me"
is any good,
they teach the tune to their crew
without telling them
who wrote it.
As soon as the words flow
out in five-part harmony,
Paul and Artie feel it—
the melody swings and
the song has wings.
After the Peptones sing it
at a school assembly,

the song starts to travel
on its own,
block by block,
neighborhood by
neighborhood,
until groups are singing it
all over Queens.
The song is a hit . . .
at least on the streets.
When someone offers to pay the boys
twenty-five dollars for it,
Paul's dad tells them
to copyright the song
with the Library of Congress.
They record an official version of it
in a Coney Island sound booth.
Neither can stop
laughing.

The Sound of Silence

Even with all the attention
"The Girl for Me" is getting,
the Peptones drift apart,
unable to find the time
to practice.
But Paul has bigger ideas
than singing
on a street corner.
Even his dad
now recognizes his talent,
letting him perform in the breaks
between his band's sets.

"Maybe we can get the song
on the radio, just the two of us?"
Paul asks Artie.
Artie gets cold feet, thinking
they're just a couple of
fourteen-year-olds
from Queens.
But Paul reminds him that
Frankie Lymon is younger than them
and he's got a hit record.
"Why not us?" he asks.
Artie can't argue with that.
"Well, I guess nothing
gets a girl's attention
like a hit song. . . ."
They make a pact:
to become radio stars

by the time they graduate
high school.

With big ideas in their heads
and a song in their hearts,
the boys ride the clanky E train
bound for Manhattan,
the fabled island where the stars
aren't in the sky
but walking on the ground.
It's a world away from Queens:
Manhattan is the place
where musicians, actors, writers,
and artists all converge,
drawn by the call of their dreams.
The boys' destination:
the Mecca of music,
the home of the hit makers,
the birthplace of gold records—
the legendary Brill Building.
Passing under the golden
churchlike arches,
the boys wander through
its hallowed hallways
lined with Number 1 hit records.
Music floats out
of closet-size rooms—
hit songs being birthed
in their presence.
"One day, we'll be writing

those songs too," whispers Artie.
Maybe we already have, thinks Paul.

Scanning the directory,
they see name after name
of music royalty—
165 music companies
waiting to discover them.
Time to show 'em
what they've got!
They knock on every door,
smile at every secretary,
sing to any cigar-smoking producer
who'll listen to them.
Day after day,
eyes roll, doors slam
in their faces.
"Thanks, but no thanks!"
The dream gets smaller,
the subway rides longer.
Paul's dad tries to warn them:
"They don't give you an A for effort
in the music biz."
After months of rejection,
they still have nothing:
no record,
no contract,
no girls screaming
their names.

Song for the Asking

Summer break.
The boys part ways,
vacationing with their families
as they try to forget
their failed attempts
at stardom.
Weeks pass.

When Paul and Artie return home,
they immediately get into
an argument
about a new song they both heard.
The tune is by a pair of brothers
from Tennessee, the Everlys.
The boys can't get that sound
out of their heads—
rockabilly harmonies?
They've never heard
anything like it.
But how did the lyrics go?
Each remembers it differently.
They try writing down
the words
but can't agree on
how the song goes.
To find out,
they take two buses
to the nearest record store
to buy the Everlys' "Hey Doll Baby."

When they finally play it,
they discover they're *both* wrong:
they've somehow managed
to combine it with
Gene Vincent's "Be-Bop-A-Lula"!

Looking at the words
they scribbled down,
they realize they've invented
something all their own—
by mistake!
Hunched over, side by side,
they write the rest of the lyrics
together.
With Paul on guitar,
they're both surprised
by how good it sounds—
just like a real record.

Scraping together seven dollars,
Paul and Artie hop a subway
to a professional studio
for one last shot at the big time.
Two voices, one guitar, one song.
Since it's recorded straight
to acetate, there are no retakes,
no room for mistakes.
They can only afford one shot—
so they better make it count.

In the studio,
it's just two boys from Queens
laying it all down,
their song, their way.
They'll give the Everlys
a run for their money.
From the first strum of his guitar,
Paul can feel the magic
coursing through his fingers.
Artie closes his eyes,
his voice in perfect sync
with his best pal.
The song pours out of them
like they're performing
in front of a packed crowd.
Electric.
They can almost hear
the audience swooning
at their every word.

When it's over,
Paul and Artie stand there,
breathless and grinning
at each other.
If nobody ever hears it,
at least they'll have a recording
just for themselves—
a snapshot of their friendship,
frozen for all time.

Last Night I Had the Strangest Dream

Lucky for them,
someone else *does* hear it.
A producer from a little label
called Big Records
happens to be in the hallway
and can't believe
what he's heard.
"I'm going to make stars
out of you!" he says.
They are all of
fifteen years old.

There's only one problem:
they need a new name.
There's already a duo
called Art and Paul.
And using their Jewish last names,
Simon and Garfunkel?
The Midwest will never go for it.
People will think they're a couple
of Borscht Belt comedians
or, worse, a law firm.
So they adopt a pretend name:
Tom and Jerry,
just like the cartoon.

A few months later,
the boys are stunned
by what's happened.
Not only is their song

playing every night
on the Moondog radio show;
it skyrockets into
a Top 10 hit in New York—
fifty thousand copies sold
in the first two days!
Now they're booked to sing
on the biggest music show
on television,
American Bandstand.
All their friends and family,
and the rest of America,
will be watching,
on Thanksgiving weekend, no less.

Down in Philadelphia,
Paul and Artie stand
onstage, frozen
in front of the cameras.
The set is still smoking
from the fireworks
of the previous performer,
the outrageous Jerry Lee Lewis.
When the host asks them
where they're from,
a nervous Paul blurts out,
"Macon, Georgia!"
because he knows rock heroes
like Jerry Lee
are all from the South.

But his little fib
doesn't matter.
Dressed in red blazers
and white shoes
and about to sing
for the first time on TV,
Paul and Artie have arrived.

When they launch into
"Hey Schoolgirl"
the teens in the crowd
jump up to dance.
The place is hopping
with squeals of delight.
Paul glances at his friend—
it wasn't long ago
they were singing alone
in Artie's basement.
Artie grins,
singing into the camera,
knowing their parents
will be watching.
Look, Ma! We're on TV!
At that moment,
everything is golden,
their song playing on the radio
alongside their idols
Elvis and the Everlys,
their teenage rock 'n' roll dreams
all coming true.

Bridge over Troubled Water

Riding high,
the boys spend their senior year
living the dream.
For once, Paul and Artie are
the most popular guys
at school.
Hounded by girls for autographs,
these neighborhood heroes
perform at record hops
and gym dances,
hit the road as a novelty act
on an all-black rock 'n' roll show,
and watch "Hey Schoolgirl" sell
over 150,000 copies.
Paul feels like everything
is turning to gold.
With more cash than he knows
what to do with,
he buys a shiny new red convertible
and an expensive electric guitar,
just like he imagines Elvis would.
They are kings of Queens
and can do no wrong —
even on the baseball field,
Paul scores the winning run
in the bottom of the 11th
by *stealing home.*

But Artie knows
from charting the rise and falls
of one-hit wonders on the radio
that sooner or later, every
bubble bursts.
Theirs bursts when Paul,
egged on by their success,
decides to pursue his old dream:
to be the Elvis of Queens.
Without telling Artie,
he records a solo record,
even asking his dad
to write a song,
hoping he'll see
how great rock 'n' roll
really is.
Only nobody wants
a Jewish Elvis.
The record flops.

Paul's failure does little
to ease Artie's hurt feelings.
Artie still feels betrayed
by his best pal.
Trying to repair their friendship,
Paul reunites with Artie
to make music again.
But those efforts fail
when their second, third,
and fourth records also flop.
Then, like some sort of karmic revenge,
Paul's fancy guitar is stolen,
and Big Records suddenly
goes bust.
When Paul's beloved sports car
catches fire
in front of Artie's house,
they watch their dreams
literally go up in flames.
Maybe the world
is trying to tell them
something.

Paul and Artie are
has-beens
at eighteen years old.

Cloudy

1959. The dream is over.
Elvis has enlisted in the army,
Little Richard enrolled in Bible school,
Jerry Lee Lewis is embroiled in scandal,
and, worst of all, Buddy Holly,
the Big Bopper, and Ritchie Valens die
in a plane crash.
Rock 'n' roll
is dead.

Like good Jewish sons,
the boys set off to pursue
respectable careers
instead of rock 'n' roll dreams.
Artie moves to Manhattan
to study architecture at
Columbia College.
Paul stays home to pursue
English lit at Queens College.
Maybe someday,
when they have proper jobs
and families,
they'll look back and say
they gave music their best shot,
and that for a few moments,
they were living the dream.

But The Voice
can't quite be silenced.
Artie wants to be an architect,

but on the side,
he joins an a cappella group
and even tries recording solo
under the names Tom Graph
and Artie Garr.
Under any name, though,
he fails to find an audience.

At school, Paul dives into poetry,
but he can't stop hearing the music
behind the words.
He meets a math major
at Queens College
named Carol
who sings and
plays piano and drums —
a kindred spirit.
Together, they form a band
and get night jobs
as song pluggers,
recording demo tunes
for other artists to sing.
At twenty-five dollars a pop,
working up
to four demos a week,
it's like going to music school.
Playing through hundreds of songs,
Paul learns how to
really make records.
When Carol decides to quit college

to pursue music,
Paul warns her, "Don't!
You'll ruin your career!"
He's shocked when, within a year,
she's written two Number 1 hits
under the name Carole King
and is suddenly making hundreds
of *thousands* of dollars.
Demoralized but wanting more,
Paul creates a few records
under different names:
Jerry Landis, Paul Kane,
even Tico and the Triumphs.
It's all mindless
teenage drivel that goes
nowhere.

Bleecker Street

As the '60s begin,
change is in the air.
College students are waking up
to social injustice and
civil rights issues
all over the country.
Down in Greenwich Village,
at Bleecker Street and MacDougal,
folk clubs spring up like protest signs,
filled with acoustic guitars and
the poetry of the people.
It's at one of these clubs
that Paul hears
a folk-singing poet
by the name of Bob Dylan.
With a voice like sandpaper,
Dylan sings blistering political songs
that hit Paul just as hard as
when he first heard Elvis.
Dylan's words set Paul's mind ablaze
with imagery of the turbulence
and absurdity of real life.
He's starting to realize there are
more important things to
write about than
teenage love.

Frustrated with New York,
Artie heads out west
to Berkeley, where the sun
shines all the time

and the young
seem golden and free.
But even there, discontent
is in the air.
Moved by the soaring voice
of a beautiful dark-haired singer
named Joan Baez,
Artie slowly gets swept up
in the anti-establishment
movement
led by the town's university.
Wanting to be part
of a bigger effort,
he starts singing folk songs
in the poetry coffee shops
around the Bay Area.
Using his voice
to express himself again
is liberating.

Feeling like his sheltered
suburban life
has limited his songwriting,
Paul graduates and takes off
for Europe in search of experience.
Alone in Paris, hitchhiking and
sleeping under bridges,
Paul sings for his supper
and widens his horizons
by exploring life
outside the States.

But the troubles back home
wrestle for his attention.
Reading about the protests
to end segregation in the South
and bolstered by Dylan's music,
Paul writes his first true adult song,
"He Was My Brother,"
about the death of a Freedom Rider,
a civil rights activist traveling by bus
into a racist Deep South.
With his mind still whirling
from music and politics,
Paul tries to fend off
pressure from his parents
to study law instead.
"Music's all very well, Paul,
but you can't make a living out of it,"
his mother says, trying
to be supportive.
Still his mother's son,
Paul reluctantly gives in,
enrolling in law school.
For a brief moment,
he justifies his decision by thinking
that being a lawyer
can help end the suffering
in the world.

Life
will lead him down
a different path.

He Was My Brother

On a crisp autumn day, 1963,
walking across the Queensboro Bridge,
Artie sees a familiar figure
heading his way.
"Paul."
"Artie."
They nod.
It has been years
since they've hung out.
Artie asks about Paul's adventures
in Europe.
Paul tells him about being
a wandering troubadour in Paris
and sleeping in a convent full of nuns.
Artie waxes on about hitchhiking
across America to be a carpenter
in California.
But he never stopped
missing New York.
"When I saw that new Dylan record,
with the cover of him walking
through the snow in the Village,
I knew I had to come back home."

Paul shares his approval
of Dylan and agrees that New York
is where it's all happening.
An awkward pause passes
and then Artie asks,
"You got any new songs?"
Paul smiles.
"A few.
Wanna hear 'em?"

Artie sits in Paul's kitchen,
where Paul plays a couple of new
acoustic tunes.
Artie listens, intrigued.
But when Paul sings "He Was
My Brother,"
a chill goes down Artie's spine.
This is not the same schoolyard
rockabilly they used to play.
This is real poetry.
When he plays it again,
Artie starts humming along,
finding his way into the song.

The third time Paul plays it,
Artie starts singing the harmony
to Paul's haunting melody.
The years slowly melt away.
The hurt of betrayal and failure
disappears.
The voices blend.
But now it's deeper than before.
Haunting and bittersweet.
Goose bumps.

Like slipping
into an old coat,
they start singing
Paul's new songs
together.
When they play them
in the stairwell
of a Jewish frat party,
the sounds of their voices echo
off the plaster walls
and the party suddenly
goes quiet.
Everyone
is listening.

America

With a gunshot,
life comes to a stop.
The assassination
of John F. Kennedy
spins Paul into a deep
depression.
It feels like the end
of hope and the beginning
of America's darkest hours.
He quits law school and
sits alone with the shades drawn.
Wrestling with his feelings,
he writes to the melancholy
darkness
like an old friend.
The words pour out.
Paul calls the song that emerges
"The Sound of Silence."
Artie is knocked out
by its visions of loneliness
and a crumbling society
numb to despair.
The song feels like a prayer
for humanity
to hold it all together.
"Where did *that* come from?"
Paul shrugs. He didn't know
he had it in him.
But Artie knows
that this song

will change
everything.

In the spring,
Paul goes to work,
trying to sell songs
to the hit makers of the day.
Visiting Columbia Records,
he finds himself pitching
to Bob Dylan's producer,
a hip black talent magnet
named Tom Wilson.
Tom digs "The Sound of Silence"
and has it in mind
for a new group, the Pilgrims.
"Actually, I sing it
with this other guy.
Maybe you'd like
to hear us?" Paul asks.
He would.

One demo later,
they are signed by one of the most
sought-after labels in America—
Columbia Records,
home to Johnny Cash, Carl Perkins,
Miles Davis, Dylan, and, now,
Simon & Garfunkel.
It's been almost seven years
since Tom and Jerry

first hit the charts.
Times have changed;
with their music pushing
new boundaries,
maybe their name
should too.
A Jewish-sounding duo
no longer seems like
such a big deal in 1964.
With a prestigious music label
behind them, and an amazing
range of new songs,
how can they lose?

But when the album
Wednesday Morning, 3 A.M.
hits the airwaves, it misses.
Badly.
Not only does nobody buy it,
but the critics dismiss them
as clean-cut college kids
trying to cash in
on the folk scene.
Veterans of failure,
Paul and Artie
strike out once again.

Homeward Bound

Fleeing,
Paul heads back to Europe,
where he feels more
at home.
He misses the smell
of coal-burning fires
and wool sweaters.
Mostly, he yearns
for a girl named Kathy
he met on last year's travels.
He settles in London,
where all he wants
is to be a busker—
playing town squares
and folk clubs
for the love of music,
not money.

Artie dives back into
finishing his studies.
Enough with show business.
Performing always wracked
his nerves anyway.
Maybe he will become an architect
or even a math teacher.
He likes being out of the spotlight
and feeling normal again.
Nothing wrong
with *not* being famous.

Meanwhile, a year after
their album failed,

a college radio station
in Gainesville, Florida,
keeps getting requests for
"The Sound of Silence."
It happens in Boston too.
Word gets back to Tom Wilson,
who is creating a new form of music
by putting Dylan's words
to electric guitar.
Why not do the same
for Simon & Garfunkel?
He asks Dylan's studio band
to lay down drums, bass,
and electric guitar
over Paul and Artie's song.
And then a funny thing happens. . . .

The revitalized song
starts to creep *up* the charts,
poking into the Top 100 in September.
By October, it's in the Top 50.
In December, Artie writes Paul.
"I think you better come home.
It's hit the Top 10!"
Paul returns to the States
fifteen months after their record failed.
He and Artie find themselves
sleeping in their old bedrooms
once again.

Kew Gardens—
just like old times.

Bookends

On New Year's Day, 1966,
bored, with nowhere to go
and nothing to do,
the boys, now men,
sit in Paul's car
outside Artie's house.
They listen to the Top 10 countdown
for a whole hour before hearing
what they've always longed to hear:
"And now for the number-one song
in America: 'The Sound of Silence'
by Simon & Garfunkel!"
They listen in disbelief, amused
that nobody recognizes
America's top act
sitting together in a car in Queens.
Artie can't help but smile.
"Those guys must be
having *so* much fun."
Paul laughs with his best friend,
amazed at this unexpected
turn of events.

But little could they know
that with just two voices
and a guitar,
they'll soon become the voices
of a generation,
outselling the Beatles
in the late '60s
and becoming cultural icons.
Soon, they'll be playing
to sold-out audiences
around the world,
eventually performing
to half a million people
in one show in their own
hometown!

At the dawn of a new year,
the new kings of the charts
have no idea that their lives
will be forever changed.
For one last moment,
sitting in the car together,
Paul and Artie
are still just
two boys
from Queens,
dreaming about
the future.

AFTERWORD

One of the most successful and influential musical duos in history, Simon & Garfunkel have sold more than a hundred million records and won ten Grammys, including a Lifetime Achievement Award. In 1990, they were inducted into the Rock and Roll Hall of Fame.

Over a five-year period, the two boys from Queens and their ethereal, harmony-drenched sound spoke to the spirit and anguish of the '60s. Their introspective and haunting albums included *Sounds of Silence; Parsley, Sage, Rosemary and Thyme; Bookends;* and *Bridge over Troubled Water. The Graduate,* a groundbreaking movie that featured their songs, pushed them into the big time. In June 1968, they were the most popular act in America, with a Number 1 single and the top *three* albums on the charts. By the early '70s, their final album, *Bridge over Troubled Water,* became the best-selling record up to that time.

They have reunited on several occasions since their 1970 breakup, most famously for 1981's Concert in Central Park, which attracted over half a million people, and a 2004 concert in Rome with an audience of over 600,000.

They each have had remarkable solo careers, filled with Number 1 hits, movie roles, and TV appearances. Even more than sixty years after they first met, the two are still in demand, selling out concerts and influencing younger musicians around the world. They last toured together in 2010.

*"This is an old friendship. We are like family. . . . We love to laugh.
We are absolutely screw-off jokesters and
have been since we met each other in the sixth grade."*
—Art Garfunkel

*"We fell in love with rock 'n' roll when we were twelve years old. . . . We were so
young that we didn't realize that this was the trip of a lifetime that we were on. . . .
I was with my oldest and my best friend; I couldn't have had a better time."*
—Paul Simon

DISCOGRAPHY

"Hey Schoolgirl," single, Big Records, 1957

Wednesday Morning, 3 A.M., Columbia Records, 1964

Sounds of Silence, Columbia Records, 1966

Parsley, Sage, Rosemary and Thyme, Columbia Records, 1966

The Graduate (soundtrack), Columbia Records, 1968

Bookends, Columbia Records, 1968

Bridge over Troubled Water, Columbia Records, 1970

Simon & Garfunkel's Greatest Hits, Columbia Records, 1972

The Concert in Central Park, Warner Brothers Records, 1982

Tom and Jerry — Their Greatest Hits, Domino Records, 1993

Live from New York City, 1967, Columbia Records, 2002

The Essential Simon & Garfunkel, Columbia Records, 2003

Old Friends — Live on Stage, Warner Brothers Records, 2004

Live 1969, Columbia Records, 2008

BIBLIOGRAPHY

This story was compiled from a variety of sources: books, magazines, newspapers, radio, video, and archival material. As much as possible, I tried to use Mr. Simon and Mr. Garfunkel as primary sources of information, collecting from more than 250 interviews and articles from the last sixty years as found on www.artgarfunkel.com, www.paul-simon.info, and in the Rock and Roll Hall of Fame archives, as well as many other online video and audio sources. Dialogue comes mostly from direct recollections from the duo, or, in a few cases, is created based on more general statements of what was discussed at a particular moment in their lives. Sometimes they had conflicting recollections between themselves or recounted events slightly differently over time; I tried to use the most repeated recollection. In every instance, I have tried to be faithful to the spirit of the moment as best I could; any errors are entirely my own.

Fornatale, Pete. *Simon & Garfunkel's* Bookends. New York: Rodale, 2007.

Garfunkel, Art. *What Is It All But Luminous: Notes from an Underground Man*. New York: Knopf, 2017.

George-Warren, Holly, ed. *Paul Simon: Words & Music*. Cleveland: Rock and Roll Hall of Fame, 2014.

Humphries, Patrick. *Paul Simon: Still Crazy After All These Years*. New York: Doubleday, 1988.

Jackson, Laura. *Paul Simon: The Definitive Biography of the Legendary Singer/Songwriter*. London: Piatkus Books, 2003.

Kingston, Victoria. *Simon and Garfunkel: The Definitive Biography*. New York: Fromm International, 2000.

Matthew-Walker, Robert. *Simon and Garfunkel*. New York: Hippocrene Books, 1984.

Morella, Joe, and Patricia Barey. *Simon and Garfunkel: Old Friends —A Dual Biography*. New York: Carol Publishing Group, 1991.

Simon, Paul. *Lyrics: 1964–2008*. New York: Simon and Schuster, 2008.

Steinberg, Susan. "Paul Simon: Born at the Right Time." WNET, 1992.

MUSICAL CONNECTIONS (in chronological order)

- Aria from *The Pearl Fishers* — Enrico Caruso (1916): When Artie was five years old, his father played him a recording by the legendary opera singer Caruso. He was blown away by the high notes and became obsessed with singing like a tenor.

- "When the Red, Red Robin Comes Bob, Bob, Bobbin' Along" — Al Jolson (1926): The first song Artie remembers singing along to with his parents. His dad realized he had perfect pitch.

- "In the Mood" — Glenn Miller (1939): One of the many popular songs Paul would play with his friend Al Kooper, sitting in with his father's band for local society gigs. Kooper would go on to a successful music career of his own.

- "You'll Never Walk Alone" from *Carousel* (1945): Artie loved Broadway musicals and sang along to the cast albums, memorizing the songs. This was one of the goose-bump-inducing songs he would sing to himself alone in the school stairwells.

- "Too Young" — Nat King Cole (1951): The song that Artie sang at the school assembly where Paul first realized Artie's great talent.

- "Anywhere I Wander" — Danny Kaye (1952): The song on which Paul displayed his newly discovered singing voice, which impressed his dad. He soon felt he could sing it well enough to perform at a school assembly.

- "Gee" — The Crows (1953): While waiting for a Yankees game to begin on the radio, Paul got his first taste of black rhythm and blues with this song. The announcer introduced it by saying he thought it was so bad that he'd eat the record if it became a hit. Paul loved it immediately, and thus began a lifelong love affair with African-American music.

- "Sh-Boom" — The Crew Cuts (1954): The first song Paul and Artie sang together in public and a great example of doo-wop.

- "Earth Angel" — The Penguins (1954): Paul found this doo-wop song to be a revelation. The combination of surreal lyrics and haunting music blew his mind. When he heard it, he tried to explain the significance to his skeptical dad. "Earth *Angel*! Don't you get it? An angel . . . from Earth!" His dad thought it was awful but still taught him the chords. It was also the first instance where Artie thought, *I want to make a record like that!*

- "Pledging My Love"—Johnny Ace (1955): This was the first record Paul ever bought. Johnny Ace was the first big rock 'n' roll star to die young, inspiring a song Paul would later write, "The Late Great Johnny Ace."

- "Mystery Train"—Elvis Presley (1955): Although "That's All Right, Mama" rocked his world, for Paul, "Mystery Train" remains the greatest song ever recorded.

- "Why Do Fools Fall in Love"—Frankie Lymon and the Teenagers (1956): The thirteen-year-old Lymon proved to the boys that young teenagers could become radio stars too.

- "Bye Bye Love"—The Everly Brothers (1957): Hearing the brothers sing changed Paul's and Artie's lives forever. This song, their biggest hit, sealed the deal, making the Everlys their model for success. When "Hey Schoolgirl" was favorably compared to the Everlys' songs, they couldn't have imagined a higher compliment. Later, Paul would say that without the Everlys, there would be no Simon & Garfunkel.

- "Great Balls of Fire"—Jerry Lee Lewis (1957): Paul and Artie had their first personal encounter with one of the great, original rock 'n' rollers when they ran into Lewis in their dressing room before their appearance on *American Bandstand.* Unfortunately, they went on after Lewis's explosive performance of "Great Balls of Fire," in which the pyrotechnics almost set the stage on fire—a tough act to follow their first time out.

- "Just to Be with You"—The Cosines (1959): Paul's other musical partnership, with Carole King, produced a series of demos—including this song—that they hoped would become hits. None did.

- "Will You Love Me Tomorrow"—Carole King (1960): When Paul's demo partner left to write full-time, this song became her first Number 1 hit, but not her last. Her success would later help push Paul to quit school and devote his life to music full-time.

- "He Was My Brother"—Paul Simon (1964): One of the first folk songs Paul wrote that was inspired by Dylan. Only a year after he penned this song about a Freedom Rider who is killed, a former classmate from Queens College, Andrew Goodman, was murdered for registering black voters in the South. His death, along with those of two other young men, became one of the most important rallying cries for justice in the civil rights era.

- "The Times, They Are a-Changin'" — Bob Dylan (1964): Paul and Artie covered this early Dylan folk tune on their first album. Later, after Dylan turned to folk rock, Tom Wilson electrified "The Sound of Silence," allegedly during the same session in which Dylan recorded what many consider to be the greatest rock song ever, "Like a Rolling Stone."

- *Meet the Beatles!* (1964): While wandering throughout England playing small clubs, Paul visited Liverpool, where he was taken to the Cavern Club to see the new band everyone was talking about: the Beatles. He and the Fab Four would later become friends.

- "Mr. Tambourine Man" — The Byrds (1965): When Tom Wilson took Dylan's folk song and electrified it with the Byrds, folk rock was born. Coincidentally, the band's leader, Roger McGuinn, was in the control room on the demo Wilson created to get the attention of Columbia Records.

- "Red Rubber Ball" — The Cyrkle (1966): In the years between "Hey Schoolgirl" and "The Sound of Silence," Paul co-wrote this song in England. It would become his first big sale as a songwriter, reaching Number 2 on the charts as sung by a band called the Cyrkle.

For Steven, my lifelong creative pal
G. N.

For Katie, Ben, and George
D. L.

First edition 2018

Library of Congress Catalog Card Number pending
ISBN 978-0-7636-8174-6

17 18 19 20 21 22 TLF 10 9 8 7 6 5 4 3 2 1

Printed in Dongguan, Guangdong, China

This book was typeset in Filosofia Grand.
The illustrations were created digitally.

Candlewick Press
99 Dover Street
Somerville, Massachusetts 02144

visit us at www.candlewick.com